With high regards
to my friend Wm. R. Wagner
– an outstanding GA –

Joseph E. [illegible]

May 25th, 1961.

TO WILL

OR

NOT TO WILL

"EVERY TESTATOR, BY THE LAW OF THE LAND, IS AT LIBERTY TO ADOPT HIS OWN NONSENSE IN DISPOSING OF HIS PROPERTY."

—*Boulle vs. Tompkins,*
5 Rdf. 472, 478.

TO WILL
OR
NOT TO WILL

BY

JOSEPH E. BRIGHT

DENNIS & CO., INC.
PUBLISHERS
BUFFALO, N. Y.
1939

TO

THE MEMORY OF

HONORABLE LOUIS B. HART

SURROGATE OF ERIE COUNTY, DEAN OF THE SURROGATES OF NEW YORK STATE, PRESIDENT OF THE NEW YORK STATE SURROGATES ASSOCIATION, MEMBER OF THE COMMISSION TO INVESTIGATE DEFECTS IN THE LAWS OF ESTATES, TO WHOM, BECAUSE OF HIS ADVICE AND COUNSEL FOR ALMOST TWENTY YEARS, I OWE A CONTINUING DEBT OF GRATITUDE, THIS VOLUME IS GRATEFULLY AND RESPECTFULLY DEDICATED.

PREFACE

THE subject of wills is interesting; the study of wills fascinating and engrossing. It is the universal method, available to anyone, to publicly and perpetually record to posterity their counsel, wishes, and desires. These recordings vary from the most profound counsel to the grossest of satire.

This author believes a brief collection of several of the many phases of wills will prove more interesting than an elaborate treatise of merely one phase of this subject, which subject is many thousands of years old.

Copies of serious wills have been purposely omitted. This author has known of many instances where testators have obtained copies of such wills and from these, attempted to draft their own will, always with disastrous results.

To the many friends, and not a few strangers who have contributed and still contribute to the author's collection of wills—sincerest thanks.

This author desires to acknowledge a debt of gratitude to the many Accountants, Attorneys, Tax Consultants and Trust Officers of various clients with whom he has worked, for their willing co-operation and the constant fund of knowledge one acquires from these contacts. Especially am I indebted to my good friend, the late Honorable Louis B. Hart, Surrogate of Erie County, and his assistants for their never-failing co-operation.

Last but not least, to my friend, Clinton Davidson, I am indebted for permission to use the phrase "Estate Planning" which he so ably coined.

—JOSEPH E. BRIGHT.

TABLE OF CONTENTS

TO WILL
OR
NOT TO WILL

HISTORY OF WILLS

A STUDY *of wills is a social study which shows man in his noblest setting. The urge to make a will is a social urge reflecting the finest impulses of human nature—impulses which operate for the benefit of others, with self-interest entirely effaced.*

Whether or not the first will was carved on tablets of stone in accordance with the concept of the above illustration, it is interesting to trace the evolution of the will through the customs of the time down to its present formal nature.

As man became more and more socially minded, he began to borrow ideas from other races with whom he came in contact. These ideas, ingrafted into our own concept of wills, form an important part of the law of wills today.

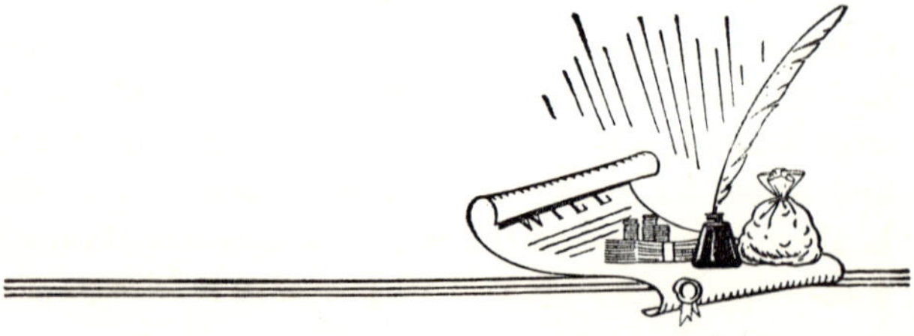

CHAPTER ONE

History of Wills

Among Savage Tribes

The origin of the right to hold property and the power to dispose of the same by will can be traced to the dawn of civilization. Ownership of property among the savage races depended upon one's ability to defend it by sheer force. In the cave-man era property passed to the one who seized it immediately after it fell out of the hands of its former custodian. Property in those days consisted of simple tools, the spear or club by which to attack, the shield by which to defend, the fishhook with which man caught a large portion of his food, the crude canoe, and perhaps some gruesome relics of victory over enemies. In that simple era there was no need for the passing of property through the medium of a will for "Might was Right."

Semi-Civilization

When man became social conscious, to the extent of recognizing the property rights of others, the need for a will began. It is to be remembered that the first dawn of civilization came upon a world in which land had no value. The movements of the nomadic tribes were limited only to where they could find pasturage and water for their flocks of sheep and goats, their herds of horses and cattle, and their caravans of camels, which constituted their chief property holdings.

From the seeds of this nomadic wandering sprang the first germ of the disposition of property after death. What could be more natural when death had terminated the journeys of the simple nomadic wanderer than for his family or next of kin to take his flocks and carry on? This marked the inception of the idea, prevalent today, that the family or next of kin have first claim on the testator's bounty. This idea has crystallized into legal restrictions on the disposition of property and is the basis for the distribution of property when no will is left.

Social Concepts Emerge

The third stage of civilization was marked by an increase in the kinds of property which were capable of ownership. Besides the herds and flocks, now grown large, slaves, for the most part, captives of war, became valuable property.

The physical impossibility of actual possession of large flocks and numerous slaves required another social concept. There then emerged the idea of constructive possession. Under this concept, property could be held although it was under the physical control of another.

Transactions in property were beginning to become common. As the idea of title to property began to take its place in an expanding society, some ceremony of transfer was thought necessary. For example, the forerunner of the modern bill of sale was the ancient ceremony of the delivery of a handful of wool to pass title to a flock of sheep. And so, with the evolution of the will, a great many formalities were required and are still required to this day.

The Roman Influence on Anglo-Saxon Wills

Historians differ as whether or not the influence of the Roman law on English wills came with the Roman Invasion or at the later period of the Norman Conquest. For our purpose, it is sufficient to notice the pronounced influence of Roman ideas on the law of English wills.

Chief among the Roman concepts was that the State had the real interest in the disposition of the property of the deceased. The family unit must be kept together in order that it might supply the men and arms necessary to the conquests of the Roman Empire. The right to transfer property freely during the lifetime of the owner was, however, fully recognized. Hence, under the Roman law, the usual mode of making a will was by an imaginary sale before witnesses, under which the testator disposed of his family and property to one who was called the Familæ Emptor, who was so named, for the sake of form, that it might appear that the testator had alienated his property during his lifetime.

The Romans had also borrowed from the Greeks the custom sanctioning the inheritance of children. From the idea of the State as an interested party in the will, and the custom sanctioning the inheritance of children, there emerged into the English law the rule of primogeniture, under which the oldest male descendant took as heir all of the decedent's real estate.

Statutory Origin of the Modern Will

The rule of primogeniture, safeguarding as it did the rights of the State to a unity of possession in the Lord of the Manor on whom the King could call for vassals to bear arms and for supplies and taxes, was thought sufficient for the State. The King, therefore, left the disposition of the personal property of a decedent to the ecclesiastical or church courts. The clergymen were the only educated people available when a will was to be made. Then too, they were usually present at the deathbed to administer the last rites of the church. The memoranda which they made of the wishes of the departing Lord of the Manor became the first wills. (See the discussion of nuncupative wills following.)

The free transfer of the personal property proved insufficient to satisfy the expanding commercial activities of the times. A way had to be found to pass lands. Lawyers soon hit upon the device of leaving the estate to an individual for the use of the purposes specified in the last will of the Lord of the Manor. This device was known as a use. It was, in many respects, akin to the modern trust. The estate would remain a unity thus satisfying the right of the King to men, supplies, and arms. The period which followed witnessed the tying up of land under these uses to such an extent that it threatened to end the free transfer of the lands of the kingdom. In 1535 the Statute of Uses was passed abolishing "uses" and converting them into full ownership. In 1540 the Statute of Wills was passed giving a full power of disposition of freehold property. In 1676 the Statute of Frauds was passed which required that devises or bequests of lands should be in writing and signed by the testator or some other person in his presence and by his direction. The modern attestation clause in your will today closely follows the language of this statute. From that day on, the law of wills became statutory.

Kinds of Wills

Nuncupative Wills

The nuncupative will has been defined as "An oral will declared by the testator before witnesses." As we have seen in this discussion of the history of wills, the curate played an important part in the development of the English will. As the increase in writing became more prevalent, these wills became obsolete, as there was usually somebody present at the bedside who could write. But even today soldiers and sailors in actual battle may make this kind of will.

Holographic Wills

A holographic will is one entirely written, dated, and signed, in the handwriting of the testator. In some states this will is valid although it is not signed or attested by witnesses.

The Mystic Will

When the French settled in Louisiana they brought with them certain legalistic ideas from the Code Napoleon. One of these was the so-called mystic will. This will is signed in the presence of the notary and seven witnesses but its contents are unknown to them. He declares the will to be his last will and testament. The will is then placed in an envelope and sealed. The envelope is then indorsed by the notary with a declaration of all the facts and acknowledged by witnesses.

Incorporation by Reference

Somewhat similar to the mystic will is the so-called incorporation by reference. In this kind of a will, the will makes reference to some existing document which is made a part of the will. For example, a will may provide that a legacy be made payable according to directions written in a book. These directions must be in existence at the time the will is signed and must not afterwards be changed.

Joint and Mutual Wills

Joint and mutual wills, if drawn by an experienced attorney, while revocable by either party during the lifetime of the other, cannot be changed after the death of one of the parties. Thus, a husband and wife, each owning property, may make a will for the purpose of distributing their property equitably among their children after death. After the death of one of the spouses, the other, after accepting the provision of the will in his or her favor, cannot dispose of the property otherwise than in accordance with the provisions of the will.

Gifts Causa Mortis

Closely resembling a gift by will is the gift called "Gift causa mortis." This is a gift made in contemplation of death and is revocable during the lifetime of the donor. This gift must be made while the donor is in peril of death and because of such peril. There must be delivery and acceptance and the gift is revocable by the donor recovering from the peril.

Conclusion

We have traced the origin of wills from its inception as a custom of the semi-savage tribe down through early England to its present statutory status. In this respect, it must be borne in mind that the statutes in every state vary in different degrees and must be thoroughly understood by the draftsman.

There has been no attempt to discuss the various perils of the will maker. Suffice it to say that the legal pitfalls of the testator who would draw his own will are as numerous as the sands on the shore of the sea. These perils can be avoided only when your will is drawn by a lawyer thoroughly familiar with the involved subject of the law of wills. If this chapter serves only to illustrate the broad scope of that subject, it will have fulfilled its purpose.

* * *

An Early American Will

Executed September 20, 1777

In the name of God, Amen. I Robert Holton of St. Mary's County in the Province of Maryland, being sick and weak of body, but of perfect sense and memory, thanks be to God for the same, and calling to mind the immortality of my body, do make this my last will and Testament in manner and form following, viz.:

> "*Item:* I give and bequeath unto my son William Holton my dwelling plantation, to him and his heirs forever, and likewise my still on his letting his brother Robert have the liberty of stilling his own liquor.
>
> "*Item:* I give unto my beloved wife and my son Robert my crops, cutt saw and my old whipsaw.
>
> "*Item:* I give unto my son Robert and my son William my two guns, my son Robert to have the small one and William the other, and likewise my two canoes giving William his choice."

LIBEL BY WILL

THESE *selections of wills, in which the testator transcended or came dangerously near transcending the law of libel and slander, throw an interesting sidelight on one phase of human nature. A few extracts follow:*

"The murderous conduct of my wife–

"To my wife I leave her lover–

"To my valet I leave the clothes he has been stealing–

"To the worst of women, unfortunately my wife–

"To the most unprincipled scoundrel–

CHAPTER TWO

Libel by Will

While, to the credit of mankind, most men in writing their last will and testament, endeavor to pass counsel, guidance, and good judgment to posterity, some have endeavored to hurl defiance at real or imaginary enemies through the pages of their last will and testament.

In 1825 an English testator left a holographic will which read:

> "I leave all of my property of every kind to my sister Mary in consequence of the cruel and murderous conduct of my wife in this illness as well as in past instances."

* * *

In New Jersey a will couched in less refined language is, nevertheless, much to the same point:

> "To my wife Anna (who is no damned good), I leave $1."

* * *

A captain of finance wrote:

> "To my wife I leave her lover, and the knowledge that I wasn't the fool she thought I was.
>
> "To my son, I leave the pleasure of earning a living. For twenty-five years he thought the pleasure was mine. He was mistaken.
>
> "To my daugher, I leave $100,000. She will need it. The only good piece of business her husband ever did was to marry her.
>
> "To my valet, I leave the clothes he has been

stealing from me regularly for ten years, also the fur coat he wore last winter while I was in Palm Beach.

"To my chauffeur, I leave my cars. He almost ruined them, and I want him to have the satisfaction of finishing the job.

"To my partner, I leave the suggestion that he take some other clever man in with him at once if he expects to do any business."

* * *

The Earl of Stafford, one of the ardent followers of James II, by his will, gave a permanent testimonial of his unhappy marriage:

> "To the worst of women, Claude Charlott de Grammont, unfortunately my wife, guilty as she is of all crimes, I leave five-and-forty brass half pence, which will buy a pullet for her supper. A better gift than her father can make her; for I have know when, having not the money, neither had he the credit for such a purchase, he being the worst of men, and his wife the worst of women, in all debaucheries. Had I known their characters, I had never married their daughter, and made myself unhappy."

* * *

Another illustration quite frequently cited in the law of libel and slander concerns a will in which a notorious libertine maliciously gave legacies in alleged compensation to certain ladies who had repulsed his advances.

Not in all instances has this form of sardonic humor been confined to men. In a very early English case, a nobleman whose wife had made serious reflections upon him in her will was successful in having the derogatory language removed.

An outstanding example of libel by will is disclosed

in a will probated in Pennsylvania in the early part of the last century, in which the testator directed that two busts be erected and placed in the Pittsburg court-house as legacies to two of the most unprincipled scoundrels who ever appeared before a court of justice.

In this instance, it appeared that the testator had a large estate which was afterwards subdivided into lots, and with the growth of the city, these lots formed a considerable portion of the business section. Therefore, in examining the title, this clause has probably been read thousands of times, and in all these years, the objects of the testator's hatred and their representatives have borne this gross imputation, for which there may have been no justification.

By a subsequent codicil, the testator carries on his motif of vengeance without the necessity of any expenditure to erect the busts. Here is the codicil:

> "In making my will I do not calculate on pleasing every expectant, my great and primary object is to please myself. I have but little to give, therefore it would be attended with the greater difficulty in mincing it out among all who might expect a little of that little."
>
> "In a former will I had directed two busts to be executed and placed in the Court House in Pittsburgh as legacies to two of the most unprincipled scoundrels who ever appeared before a court of justice; one of them is dead in reality, and the other dead to all feelings of moral principle. I now decline a continuation of that appropriation and direct it to be applied to a tombstone and epitaph for myself as follows, viz.:
>
> Adamson Tanehill
> Was born the 23rd of May, 1750.
> Died
> ____ of ____, 18__ Aged ____ years.

"He served his country as an officer during the American Revolution, with the confidence of his superiors, &c., but in the year of 1798, his character was assailed unjustly by the slander of unprincipled men and virulence of Party.

Has left this world with the hope of a better.

Farewell vain world: I've seen enough of thee,
And am now careless what thou sayest of me—
Thy smiles I court not, nor thy frown I fear,
My cares are past, my head lies quiet here—
What faults you saw in me take care to shun—
And look at home, enough's there to be done.
False swearing and vile slander can't reach me here,
Of each, when living, I had my share."

* * *

There are frequent illustrations of occasions in which the testator probably had no intention of reflecting on the character or morals of living persons. For example, the following will from Texas in the Dutch vernacular may have been the result of thrifty caution on the part of the testator:

"I am writing of my will mineself and des lawyir vant he should have to much money he ask to many answers about the famly. first think I vant I dont vant my brother oscar to get a g— thing I got he is a mumser he done me out of forty dollars fourteen years since.

"I vant it that hilda my sister she gets the north sixtie akers of at where i am homing it now i bet she dont get that loafer husband of her to brake twentje akers next plowing the gonoph work. she cant have it if she lets oscar live on it i want i should have it back if she does.

"tell moma that six hundret dollars she has been looking for for ten years is berried from the bakhouse behind about ten feet down she better let little frederick do the digging and count it when he comes up.

"pastor lucknitz can have three hundret dollars if he kisses the book he vont preech no more dumhead talks about politiks, he should a roof put on the meeting-house with and the elders should the bills look at.

"moma should the rest get but i vant it so that adolph should tell her what not she should do so no more slick irishers sell her vaken cleaners they noise like hell and a broom dont cost so much.

"i vant it that mine brother adolph be my evecter and i vant it that the judge should please make adolph plenty bond put up and watch him like hell adolph is a good business man but only a dumkoph would trust him with a busted pfennig.

"i vant dam sure that schliemial oscar dont nothing got tell adolph . he can have a hundret dollars if he prove judge oscar dont get nothing that dam sur fix oscar."

* * *

To those exceptional persons who would indulge in this pastime of defaming others through the medium of their wills, here is a word of caution. In a number of instances, the objectionable language was ordered removed before the will was allowed to be probated, and in others, heavy damages for libel have been recovered against the estate.

HUMOROUS WILLS

TO *really live requires laughter, and people everywhere have had their spirits lifted by mirth. Perhaps one of the strangest places to look for humorous items would be in the wills of testators who must consciously face the contemplation of death when they write their wills, but nevertheless, there are many incidents of pure humor glancing out from the pages of many wills with provisions such as*

—"My overdraft on my bank"

—The "Buffalo Turn-verein" shall have first claim on my ashes"

—"Wrap me in a horse blanket and put me in a pine box."

CHAPTER THREE

Humorous Wills

One testator directed that no woman be present at his funeral. If his wife survived him, he would be cremated; otherwise, he would be buried in the ordinary way.

* * *

A merchant recognizing the uncertainties of life, gave the following directions to his lawyer:

> "Make my will so my overdraft at the bank goes to my wife—she can explain it. My equity in my car to my son—he will have to go to work to keep up the payments. Give my good will to the supply house—they took some awful chances on me and are entitled to something. My equipment you can give to the junk man—he has had his eye on it for several years. I want six of my creditors for pall bearers—they have carried me so long they might as well finish the job."

* * *

A Frenchman, declaring the French to be "a nation of dastards and fools," left his fortune to the poor of London, and further ordered that his body should be launched into the sea a mile from the English coast.

* * *

The love of the French people for the culinary arts is reflected in the following will providing that a new cooking recipe should be pasted on the testator's tomb each day.

A French lawyer left $10,000 to a local madhouse, declaring that it was simply an act of restitution to his clients.

* * *

A rich American left every dollar he possessed to a girl he used to watch in the theatre. He did not know her, and the only reason he made the bequest was that her turned-up nose amused him.

* * *

Perfect indeed would be the legatee who could qualify under the following conditions: No one could benefit who was an idler, a sluggard, a profligate, a drunkard, or a gambler. The use of liquor and tobacco would deprive a legatee of his portion. He was also debarred from entering any bar-room or porter-house, from getting married before the age of twenty-five, or even from not having risen, breakfasted and got ready for business by nine o'clock in the morning.

* * *

How deep the sentiment of a lovely lady who directed, in her will, that tobacco should be planted over her grave, and that the weed, nourished by her dust, might be smoked by her bereaved lovers.

* * *

A cremation clause provided for the "ashes to be blown off the Electric Tower, and if they won't stand for that, bottle up same so that it won't explode and place it in the Musician's Headquarters or Eagles. Be sure to have a band. No ceremony only of the Eagles, and wish to be buried from there. No expensive casket."

* * *

The same testator provided that "all my music, including my music trunk to my friend H. D. Music all up to date. McD. to do the honors, taking charge of the funeral. Old clothes to the poor. Savage gun in big trunk to A. F. Big trunk to D. N. H. D. to make a few dysentery remarks before cremation. Anyone to lead the procession."

* * *

Another will providing for cremation specified: "My body shall be cremated as the enclosed receipt, August 12, 1886, says. For this purpose my body shall be dressed in the garment as it lays in my bedroom cupboard, marked "my last toilette."

* * *

The funeral rights shall be conducted as plain and reasonable as possible. No "Pfaffe": Priest, Pastor, Reverend, Rabbi, or however these idlers style up themselves, is allowed to participate or be present.

* * *

The "Buffalo Turn-verein" shall have the first claim upon the ashes.

* * *

After the incineration of my body, resp. as soon as my body is under fire in the furnace, my friends are invited to a "salamander" with lunch at Turn Hall, or any other convenient place at the expense of $20.

* * *

Should, at this occasion, anybody either at the house or at the crematory, or at the banquet, wish to sing, please execute *only jolly songs.*"

* * *

A Cincinnati gardener wrote:

> "Knowing that all men must go sooner or later to that great beyond, so I ______, of right mind,

do make my will and last request. After my debts are paid, I give all that is left of my estate to my beloved wife. I give it to her same as I would reach in my pocket and give my little girl a dime.

"She is not to give any bond or go through any Court form, only to have my will recorded in the Probate Court so she can have power to sign checks as I would be on earth.

"Do not spend much money on my funeral as I would be just as well off if I was wrapped in a horse blanket and put in a pine box. Save all you can, because you will miss that week's pay I used to bring home."

* * *

One testator left all his property to the devil. The name of the legatee appeared in capital letters throughout the will. The inference was that the testator wished to make a good impression upon him, with an eye to securing indulgence when they met.

* * *

An elderly gentleman, who knew something of law, lived in an Irish village where no solicitor had ever penetrated, and was in the habit of arranging the disputes of his neighbors and making their wills. At an early hour one morning, he was aroused from his slumbers by a loud knocking at the gate, and putting his head out of the window, he asked who was there.

"It's me, yer Honor,–Paddy Flaherty, I could not get a wink of sleep thinking of the will I have made."

"What's the matter with the will?" said the amateur lawyer.

"Matter indeed!" replied Pat; "sure I've not left myself a three-legged stool to sit down upon!"

* * *

This is the Last Will and Testament of an attorney, a resident of Buffalo:

First: I give and bequeath as follows:

To Wm. J. S., Esquirt	$500.00
J. M. (Ex-Constable, damned scoundrel et cetery)	100.00
D. G. (Ex-Wrestler & Ancient Friend)	50.00
P. S. 7 Street (Ancient friendship)	100.00
M. A. G., Lawyer (Unfortunately)	75.00
H. W. P., Lawyer (regrettably)	25.00
A. W., Gent. (In token of adolescent days in the law)	10.00
Wm. P. (ancient friendship)	150.00
J. C. (In remembrance of our boyhood, happy days. Also as a solatium for the horrible suffering & torture endured by Jimmy in Canadian Jails—consequent upon Gen. J. O'N. Fenian Raids, in 1866)	10.00
N. S. H. "Old Succotash"	50.00
C. J. T., A reformed blackguard	10.00
A. F. C., "Oldest Inhabitant"	15.00
F. J. F. C. (In remembrance of her first appearance upon the world stage)	25.00
A. K. S. (dehors feathers)	50.00
Mrs. E. S. J. in token of my regard for a real woman	25.00
Mrs. A. M. F. (Prior to August, 1924, it was my intention to bequeath $2000 with the purpose of doubling the same in due course of time, but since then,—"it can't be did." "It goes against the grain," and I am again impelled to take satisfaction by "cutting down" the appropriation to	$2.00

(Hinc illae Lacrimae)

To cover any loss, damage, detriment consequent upon my demise—as a boarder & Lodger 150.00 (This shall be deemed and take as "liquidated damages," and not as a penalty as suggested by Corkscrew Twinn)

LITERARY AND POETIC WILLS

ONE *of the most beautiful pieces of fiction in American literature appears in the will of Charles Lounsberry, reported in full in this chapter. This will was written by a Chicago lawyer of the old school and has been published widely in magazines and periodicals. No one can read this will without sensing the esthetic ideals of the writer. His language is clear and beautiful, and appeals to all lovers of literature.*

Poetic wills, some of them containing flashes of humor, are also included.

CHAPTER FOUR

Literary and Poetic Wills

THE WILL OF CHARLES LOUNSBURY

IN the name of God, amen. I, Charles Lounsbury, being of sound and disposing mind and memory, do now make and publish this my Last Will and Testament, in order, as justly as I may, to distribute my interests in the world among succeeding men.

"And first, that part of my interests which is known among men and recognized in the sheep-bound volumes of the law as my property, being inconsiderable and of none account, I make no account of in this my will.

"My right to live, it being but a life estate is not at my disposal, but, these things excepted all else in the world I now proceed to devise and bequeath.

"Item—And first, I give to good Fathers and Mothers, but in trust for their children, nevertheless, all good little words of praise and all quaint pet names, and I charge said parents to use them justly but generously as the needs of their children shall require.

"Item—I leave to children exclusively, but only for the life of their childhood, all and every, the dandelions of the fields and the daisies thereof, with the right to play among them freely, according to the custom of children, warning them at the same time against thistles. And I devise to children the yellow shores of creeks and the golden sands beneath the waters thereof, with the dragon flies that skim the surface of said waters, and the odors of the willows that dip into the said waters, and the white clouds that float high over the giant trees.

"And I leave to children the long, long days to be merry in, in a thousand ways, and the Night and the Moon and the train of the Milky Way to wonder at, but subject, nevertheless, to the rights hereinafter given to lovers; and I give to each child the right to choose a star that shall be his, and I direct that the child's father shall tell him the name of it, in order that the child shall always remember the name of that star after he has learned and forgotten astronomy.

"Item—I devise to boys jointly all the useful idle fields and commons where ball may be played, and all snow-clad hills where one may coast, and all streams and ponds where one may skate to have and to hold the same for the period of their boyhood. And all meadows, with the clover blooms and butterflies thereof; and all woods, with their appurtenances of squirrels and whirring birds and echoes and strange noises; and all distant places which may be visited, together with the adventures there found, I do give to said boys to be theirs. And I give to said boys each his own place at the fireside at night, with all pictures that may be seen in the burning wood or coal to enjoy without let or hindrance and without any incumbrance of cares.

"Item—To lovers I devise their imaginary world, with whatever they may need, as the stars of the sky, the red, red roses by the wall, the snow of the hawthorn, the sweet strains of music, or aught else they may desire to figure to each other the lastingness and beauty of their love.

"Item—To young men, jointly, being joined in a

brave, mad, crowd, I devise and bequeath all boisterous, inspiring sports of rivalry. I give to them the disdain of weakness and undaunted confidence in their own strength. Though they are rude and rough, I leave to them alone the power of making lasting friendships and of possessing companions; and to them exclusively I give all merry songs and brave choruses to sing, with smooth voices to troll them forth.

"Item—And to those who are no longer children or youths or lovers, I leave Memory, and I leave to them the volumes of the poems of Burns and Shakespeare, and of other poets, if there are others, to the end that they may live the old days over again freely and fully, without tithe or diminution; and to those who are no longer children or youths or lovers I leave, too, the knowledge of what a rare, rare world it is.

Charles Lounsbury."

* * *

In 1770, there was admitted to probate at the Deanery Court at York, England, the poetical will of one William Hickington.

"This is my last will,
I insist on it still,
To sneer on and welcome,
And e'en laugh your fille,
I, William Hickington,
Poet of Pocklington,
Do give and bequeath,
As free as I breathe,
To thee, Mary Jarum,
The Queen of my Harum,
My cash and my cattle,
With every chattel,
Come heat or come cold,
Sans hindrance or strife,
Though thou are not my wife.
As witness my hand,

Just here as I stand,
The twelfth of July,
In the year Seventy."

* * *

The Lawyer's Will

I give and bequeath,
To Heaven my soul,
And leave to the earth
My body to hold.

To Heaven in fee
Do I give my soul,
To keep it forever,
And keep the whole.

But I leave my body
To the earth in trust,
To account to Heaven,
For its proceeds of dust.

For the natural life
Of this planet I leave
My body to Earth
And afterwards give

The remainder to Heaven,
In fee, like the soul,
To continue forever,
The two a joint whole.

A vested remainder
Of my body I give
To Heaven, so that it
Gets all I've to give.

For having already
The soul in possession,
'Twill need but the body
To have all the rest of me.

And should this my testament
Fail of effect,
And anything lapse
Of this my bequest,

That Heaven can't take,
Or that Hell gets a part
Of my personal property
By any default,

Good God if the Devil
Comes for his share
On the ground of the evil
I've done or have dared

I pray my effects
May descend not by law;
For if they don't go by will
The Devil'll get all.

Codicil

And should I perchance
Have title alone
To the life that's now ending
And soon to be gone–

Should life in the future
That's so full of danger,
And is after all but a
Contingent remainder,

Not pass by devise,
But determine with me,
And my life estate prove
The whole of the fee–

Then dying a bankrupt,
My will's not worth proving,
And chiefly the Devil
Will suffer by losing.

* * *

Another poetic will was probated in Texas.

"All my earthly goods I have in store
To my dear wife I leave for evermore.
I freely give; no limit do I fix.
This is my will, and she my executrix,
To serve without bond."

BEQUESTS THAT FAILED

IN *this chapter the author brings to your attention certain celebrated wills which have been defeated by mistakes or lack of vision on the part of the testator.*

Herein are treated bequests, such as "Sailors sailing on sailing-whaling vessels."

"To indigent travelers going westward in covered wagons."

Mistakes which have produced strange results are also discussed in this chapter as well as interesting sidelights on the lay attitude toward the will.

CHAPTER FIVE

Bequests that Failed

THE power is not given to mortal men to look through the fog which veils the future heights of progress towards which mankind marches with relentless steps.

Today's need may be tomorrow's abundance. What was common only yesterday may, on the early morrow, be much sought after as a rare antique.

This process, which is so noticeable in a scientific world, has played havoc with the kindly intent of many a testator. An outstanding example of this is the bequest made by a wealthy New England shipowner in the days preceding navigation by steam. In his will, he made elaborate provision for maintaining a home for indigent sailors of *sailing-whaling* vessels. With the advent of navigation by steam, the sailing vessel became obsolete.

The net result of this economic change is that a fund amounting to several million dollars cannot now be devoted to the specific purposes desired by the testator.

* * *

Equally futile, but coming from another section of the country, was the bequest of a Missouri pioneer who limited the beneficiaries of a trust to indigent travelers going westward in covered wagons. The covered wagon, however picturesque, has given way to other and more speedy means of transportation, and the westward ho of immigrants going westward to seek their fortune has become merely an historic cry of a period now gone, but the fund remains, although there is no possibility of expending it in accordance with the intent of the testator.

* * *

One principle of the law of wills is to the effect that the court will not go beyond the plain language of the will to discover the intent of the testator. For example, if the will leaves property to "My nephew Jack," and there is a nephew by that name, the courts will not admit evidence attempting to show that the testator really meant to leave the property to nephew James and unintentionally called him Jack. This apparently simple and necessary rule has, in a few isolated cases, led to strange results.

Consider the will of one, Nathaniel Tucker of Milton, Massachusetts, who made his will in 1838. A seafaring man all his life and one who had amassed a considerable fortune from the sea, he turned his thoughts during his declining years towards the welfare of seamen. He became interested in a society which was called, *"The American Seaman's Friends Society."* He corresponded with this society and subscribed to its various publications, one of which was called *"The Sailor's Magazine."* The scrivener whom he employed to write his will was under the impression that the legal name of this society was *"The Seaman's Aid Society,"* and he so informed the testator. In consequence of this erroneous information, the bequest was made in the will to *"The Seaman's Aid Society."*

After his death, it was discovered that there were two distinct organizations. The litigation which resulted finally reached the Supreme Judicial Court of Massachusetts. Chief Justice Shaw, one of America's great legal scholars, delivered the opinion of the court (Tucker v. Seaman's Aid Society, 48 Mass. (7 Met.) 188). The court found that "The Seaman's Aid Society" was composed of, and managed largely by females (of whom as a class, the testator had a profound contempt), and that there was no evidence that the testator ever knew that such an organization was in existence. On the other hand, the interest and sympathy of the testator in the relief and improvement of seamen had been extended over, and fostered by, the publications of the *"American Seaman's Friends Society,"* and that it was his intention to make the bequest to the *"American Seaman's Friends Society."* But notwithstanding this clear intent of the testator, on the face of the will all was plain and clear. Its written provisions could not be controlled or altered by the court, and the *"Seaman's Aid Society"* received the property.

Thus, a considerable fortune passed to an institution of whose existence the testator was unaware, of whose managament the testator would not have trusted, and notwithstanding his intent that an entirely different organization should benefit from his charity.

* * *

However strong the intent of the testator to make a valid disposition of his property, if the legal formalities are not complied with, it is of no effect.

A will drawn by a Kentucky justice of the peace, which was couched in inarticulate phrases and which contained after the signature of the witnesses the following: "Certificate." "This is to certify that the above authentic and valid will this ----- day ----- of

----- was drawn by me ------ justice of the peace. This illustrates the extent to which incompetent draftsmen go."

* * *

A new way to ignore law has been found. A leading business man submitted to his lawyer a holographic will with absolute assurance that it was in proper form. One of its provisions was as follows: "Should there be a law at the time of my death directing how a child by a first marriage should share in its father's estate, I hereby direct that said law be entirely ignored, unless it conforms with the following request."

The distribution of the estate would not have been affected by this clause, as his wife was the principal legatee, yet the instance furnishes an interesting sidelight on a successful business man's attitude towards statutory regulations.

Numerous are the instances in which bequests to charities have failed because of faulty draftsmanship. One great pit-fall which has resulted in literally thousands of wills being declared invalid is the requirement that a definite beneficiary must be designated.

For example, in Rhode Island a provision in a will that the testator's house shall be kept open for the entertainment of ministers and others traveling in the service of truth was held invalid. A moment's reflection will show that the beneficiaries under this request cannot be ascertainable and hence the provision is invalid as a violation of the rule requiring a definite existing beneficiary.

In North Carolina a will which contained the bequest to some promising young man of good talents and of the Baptist order, to be selected by the testator's executors, was held void because of the uncertainty as to the object of the testator's bounty.

So strict has been the rule that in one case, at least in New York, a bequest setting apart the income from a fund to be applied for the purchase of shoes for poor children attending the parochial schools was held invalid for the same reason—as indefinite.

It would indeed take a skilled legal mind to avoid a mistake such as the one which rendered this will invalid.

* * *

Executors sometimes have queer constructions of provisions in wills, as witnessed by the following doggerel:

"When Abe met Jacob on the street,
He paused a moment him to greet,
And on his shirt-front spied a rare
Large diamond like the sun's strong glare—
A diamond whose prodigious size
Could surely dazzle any eyes.
And in a most inquisitive tone
Said, 'Jakie, where you got dot stone?'
Said Jake, 'Why Abie, don't you know
A will was made by poor, dead Moe?
And, confidential, what is more,
It says I am executor,
And in dat will it plainly stands
(which 'tween us, Abe is my commands),
Dat I, executor, should try
For toosent dollar quickly buy
A beautiful memorial stone,
For, unberufen, him whose gone.'
He touched that diamond's polished zone,
Then slyly said in pride-drenched tone,
'And confidential,
Dot's
the
stone!' "

QUAINT AND CURIOUS WILLS

IN *the chapter will be found a collection of quaint and curious bequests of which the following provision is a glittering example. The will provided that two drumheads were to be made of the testator's skin. Upon one was to be inscribed, "Pope's Universal Prayer," and on the other the "Declaration of Independence."*

The mathematician's will, in which the crushing power of compound interest is ably demonstrated, will make interesting reading to the mathematically inclined.

The ghost's will, with the incidents accompanying it, may make thrills creep up and down your spine.

The drunkard's will, and various other quaint and curious provisions, are treated in this chapter.

CHAPTER SIX

Quaint and Curious Wills

ONE testator left his body to the anatomical museum of Harvard, with the gruesome provision that two drumheads were to be made of his skin. Upon one was to be inscribed Alexander Pope's "Universal Prayer," and on the other the "Declaration of Independence;" and then they were to be presented to the testator's distinguished friend, the drummer of Cohasset. This presentation was subject to the condition that on the 17th of June at sunrise every year, the drummer should beat "on the drumheads at the foot of Bunker Hill the spirit-stirring strains of Yankee Doodle."

THE MATHEMATICIAN'S WILL

One of the most unusual wills in this collection reflects the life work of the testator, a teacher in arithmetic, who was by birth a Frenchman. It was probated over one hundred and fifty years ago in a little village in England. The will disposed of the modest sum of twenty-two pounds. It evidences, however, uncanny powers of calculation.

The preface to this will teaches a lesson in prudent investment which cannot be too highly recommended to the present generation.

> "This sum proceeded originally from a present which was made me from my much honored grandfather when I entered the eighth year of my

age. At that age he had taught me the principles of writing and calculation. After having shown me that capital, with its accumulated interest of five per cent would at the end of one hundred years amount to more than one hundred and thirty-one times the original sum, and seeing that I listened to this lecture with the greatest attention, he took twenty-four livres (a guinea) out of his pocket, and addressed me with an enthusiasm which is still present to my mind.

" 'My child,' he said, 'remember whilst thou livest, that with economy and calculation nothing is impossible to man! Here are twenty-four livres which I give thee. Take them to a merchant in our neighborhood, who will place them in trade, out of regard for me. Every year thou shall add the interest to the principal. At thy death thou shall employ the produce in good works.' "

At the time of writing his will the testator was in his seventy-first year, and by strictly following the advice of his grandfather, the twenty-four livres had grown to five hunded. A brief summary of the disposition of this sum follows: It was to be divided into five equal portions and each portion put out at interest in the same way as the original gift. The testator's directions as to the disposition of these sums follows:

"First fund: After one hundred years the first sum would amount to thirteen thousand, one hundred livres (5,822 pounds). From this fund a sum of one thousand, five hundred pounds was to be given for the best essay proving the lawfulness of putting money out to interest. Three gold medals were to be given and the rest of the fund spent in printing and giving wide distribution to the essays.

"Second fund: The second sum after two hundred years would amount to 1,700,000 livres (756,500 pounds). This fund was to be used in establishing perpetual yearly prizes of one thousand livres each, these prizes to be as follows:

15 prizes for the most distinguished virtuous actions.
15 prizes for the best works of science and literature.
10 prizes for arithmetical solutions.
10 prizes for agricultural improvements.
10 prizes for masterpieces in fine arts.
10 prizes for athletics.
10 prizes for religious dissertations.

"Third fund: The third sum after three hundred years would be increased to two hundred and twenty-six million livres (10,057,000 pounds). This sum was to be used as follows: One hundred and ninety million livres to establish five hundred banks in France for lending money without interest. Thirty million livres to found museums at Paris, Lyons, Bordeaux, Rouen, Reenes, Lille, Nancy, Tours, Dijon, Toulouse, Aix, and Grenoble. Each of these museums was to be endowed so that each could support a staff of forty literary men and artists of superior merit. As to these, the testator with a glint of humor directed 'at the time of meals shall be divided into four tables, that their repast may be cheerful without being too noisy.' Free libraries, galleries of natural history, concert halls, theatres, free lectures are to be maintained from this fund.

"Fourth fund: The fourth fund, amounting with interest, at the end of four hundred years to thirty thousand millions of livres is to be employed in building one hundred towns, to accommodate 159,000 inhabitants in the most agreeable locations in France. The testator realized that all the specie in Europe would not reach this amount, therefore, he directs that when necessary, real estate may be bought.

"Fifth fund: The accumulations of five hundred years would increase this fund to four mil-

> lion millions of livres (136,000,000,000 pounds). A portion of this fund, eighteen thousand millions, is to be used in paying off the national debt of France and England with this condition: 'The kings shall be entreated to order the comptrollers to undergo an examination in arithmetic before they enter upon their office.' "

The comments of the testator in regard to the national debts of these nations make interesting reading:

> "It may be seen that I reckon that both these national debts will be doubled in this period; not that I have any doubts of the talents of certain ministers to increase them much more, but their operations in this way are opposed by an infinity of circumstances which lead me to presume that these debts cannot be more than doubled. Besides, if they amount to a few thousands of millions more, I declare that it is my intention that they should be entirely paid off, and that a project so laudable should not be deferred for a trifle more or less."

The relationship between France and England at that time was far from friendly. The testator makes this conciliatory statement:

> "I beg that the English would not refuse this slight mark of the remembrance of a man, who was indeed born a Frenchman, but who sincerely esteemed their nation. I earnestly desire that, as an acknowledgment of this legacy, the English nation will consent to call the French their neighbors, and not their natural enemies, that they may be assured that Nature never made man an enemy to man; and that national hatreds commercial prohibitions, and above all wars constantly produce a monstrous error in calculations."

The further legacies to be paid from this fund show that the testator was years ahead of his times in social thinking. They include bequests for the following purposes:

"1. The encouragement of peace.
"2. The extinction of state lotteries.
"3. The abolishment of useless public offices.
"4. Increase in salaries of ministers, but on condition that the clergy forego their fees for saying masses.
"5. The cultivation of wild lands.
"6. The advancement of education.
"7. Public work projects. Here, all who demand work were to have it.
"8. The establishment of hospitals.
"9. The furtherance of employment.
"10. The proper remuneration of women."

The will concludes with the following benediction:

> "May the success of the establishments cause one day a few tears to be shed on my grave! But above all, may the example of an obscure individual kindle the emulation of patriots, princes, and public bodies; and engage them to give attention to this new but powerful and infallible means of serving posterity, and contributing to the future improvement and happiness of the world."

The Drunkard's Will

If you have some bad habits, they may be brought to light, but will hardly affect your will. You may indulge in various brands of "oh! be joyful," but if you are sober when you make your will and are careful to have that fact provable, your testamentary capacity may be saved. You may lie about your property when pestered with gratuitous advice about what to do with your money, or, like a certain old woman, you may take a mischievous delight in deceiving your nieces and nephews, promising your estate to them all; but when it is found out that you have deceived them all but one, it will not affect your testamentary capacity.

Speaking of a drinking man, he has the testamentary capacity, though frequently drunk, if he makes his will when sober. The following will illustrates how a certain testator succeeded in avoiding any trouble of testamentary capacity. It is given verbatim, except a fictitious name has kindly been substituted. The italics are the testator's.

> "I, Richard Roe, of Adams County, do hereby in my own handwriting declare this to be my last will and testament, hereby revoking every and all other by me at any time made and there are several, each and every one of which I do now most solemnly declare and say was made and executed when I was too *drunk* to know or realize the acts or the effects of the papers I was executing, particularly one in the hands of ________. If not absolutely *drunk* at the execution of the said wills, my mind, enfeebled and debilitated by the excessive use of liquors, was incapable of judging between *right* and *wrong*, wherefore I do now and hereby give, devise, and bequeath," etc.

The Ghost Will

A strange story is told in connection with the finding of a will that was filed in the Probate Court of an Ohio county. The brother of the deceased tells the following marvelous story as to the manner of finding the will. He says that on Tuesday night, June 17, 1885, he and his family could get but little rest owing to unaccountable noises in the house. Doors slammed and peculiar knockings disturbed their slumbers. Towards morning Mr. B. got up to investigate the mystery. A rummaging sound seemed to issue from one room, and he opened the door and looked in and was astounded to see what appeared to be the form and face of his brother Dan bending over a desk in the corner. He summoned courage to ask him what was wanted, and the reply was, "those papers." The form was luminous, and when it had uttered these words it faded before his eyes and disappeared. Mrs. B. was, of course, told the story and she was very careful to stay away from that particular room. When her husband returned she was a badly frightened woman and told him that she had heard peculiar sounds in that room during the day, as though caused by lifting the desk lid and letting it fall. He then resolved to make an examination, and after rummaging through the desk the will was found. The will itself is a literary curiosity.

> "Bucyrus Crawford County, May the 21 1885, this is my last will and testament after my dith.
>
> "first my detts are god to be paid then the car photograph car and the machinery goyes to will n B. and my cloth (clothes to J. P. B. and to L Mollenhaph Absolom is to git ten dolares i place of cloth (clothes) he cand ware eney of them and will is to run the Bisness if it pays him and I think it will Misses R. gits ten dolars as a preusent Kate B. gits five Ela B. gits two and the rest to be dividet equall among the three Brothers and sister or thare ares is eney thing left for them i dont want youance to quarl and to fight about it and git noting do it up in pes and good will and stay friends i almost for god my girl magie B. is to have ten dolares she was my girl and so i will close
>
> Daniel B. seal
>
> We the under sined agnalage thahat Dannel B. was in his sound mind and have seen him sinc his name
>
> J R K——
> & Christ R——"

A will without punctuation marks appears in a Pennsylvania case, as follows:

"In the Name of God I Samuel Eddinger
of Moore Township County of Northamton
State of Penn Do make this my Last will
and testament as follows
that is to Say my Disire
my son John he Shall have one
thousand Dollars in Advance before
any of the heirs Shall have any money
from my Estate personal property
first my Son John Shall Setle up all
my Depts funeral Expenc &c
till all is paid
my Son John he shall setle
my personal property as soon
it is Posibile
he shall pay the of the money from
my personal goods the half of
the money to my Daughter Magret and
what is Left from the Balence of
the Thousand Dollars he tookt of for himself
my Son John Shall pay to my
Daughter Magret an Annually one a
Hundred and twenty five Dollars for her
Natural Life time or as Long she
will Liv in this World
And my Son John he shall have
all my real Eastate for his own
property as Soon my Daughter is Deased
my Son John Shall not pay any Longer
Dowery not to her heirs and to nobody
interest it be Stopt"

* * *

Various quaint and curious provisions have found their way into wills.

One testator, an English nobleman, provided that

he should have two resting places. Under the provision of his will, after a certain period had elapsed, his body was to be exhumed and buried on an island where legend affirms are buried several thousand saints.

* * *

An Englishman left his body to a hospital with instructions that his skeleton should be prepared and cleaned, and his head preserved entire, and that he should, when thus treated, preside at the meetings of the hospital directors.

* * *

A German bequeathed his effects to a poor man, whom he intensely disliked, on condition that he always wore linen underclothes, without any additional underclothing, the tendency of linen underclothes to scratch being considered, by the testator, as a punishment.

* * *

An attendant at a theatre left this remarkable direction: "My head to be separated from my body, duly macerated and prepared, then to be employed to represent the skull of Yorick in the play of 'Hamlet.' "

* * *

Grim sarcasm is apparent in the following will:

> "Imprimis: As for the soul, I do confess I have often heard men speak of the soul, but what may be these same souls, or what their destination, God knoweth; for myself, I know not. Men have likewise talked to me of another world, which I have never visited, nor do I even know an inch of the ground that leadeth thereto. When the King was reigning, I did make my son wear a surplice, being desirous that he should become a Bishop, and for myself I did follow the religion

of my master; then came the Scotch who made me a Presbyterian, but since the time of Cromwell, I have become an Independent. These are, methinks, the three principal religions of the kingdom,—if any of three can save a soul, to that I claim to belong; if, therefore, my executors can find my soul, I desire they will return it to him who gave it to me.

"Item: I give my body, for it is plain I cannot keep it, as you see the chirurgeons are tearing it in pieces. Bury me, therefore, I have lands and churches enough for that. Above all, put not my body beneath the church porch, for I am, after all, a man of birth, and I would not that I should be interred there where Colonel Pride was born.

"Item: I will have no monument, for then I must needs have an epitaph and verses over my carcase; during my life I have had enough of these."

He goes on to say his last compliments to some of his friends:

"Item: I give nothing to my Lord Saye, and I do make him this legacy willingly, because I know that he will faithfully distribute it unto the poor.

"Item: I bequeath to Thomas May, whose nose I did break at a mascarade, five shillings. My intention had been to give him more; but all who shall have seen his 'History of the Parliament' will consider that even this sum is too large.

"Item: I give to the Lieutenant-General Cromwell one of my words, the which he must want, seeing that he hath never kept any of his own."

* * *

An English politician made the following bequests:

"To Mr. George Grey, Secretary to the Presidency, I bequeath all my sincerity; to Mr. Simon Drose, Writer to the Secretary's office, all my modesty; to Mr. Henry Higgenson, also of the Secretary's office, all the thoughts I hope I shall die possessed of; to Mr. Thomas Forbes, all the worldly assurance which I had when I had taken a cheerful glass, though in fact a doleful cup."

* * *

A Scotch dissenting minister, bequeathed a sum of money to his chapel at St. Ives to provide: "Six Bibles every year, for which six men and six women are to throw dice on Whit Tuesday after the morning service, the minister kneeling the while at the South end of the Communion table, and praying God to direct the luck to his glory."

* * *

The dread of being buried alive has resulted in some elaborate precautions. One testator directed that four days after death two skillful surgeons were to be paid five pounds each to perform such an operation on his body as would prevent the possibility of his coming to life in his coffin.

* * *

One testator directed that he be not buried in the family vault, his body was to be watched until decomposition set in.

* * *

One millionaire was so anxious about his corpse that he would not let it be left in the dark. Not only did he provide for the vault to be lighted by electricity, but he also ordered the coffin to be so illuminated.

* * *

Difficulties of testators and heirs might be thought sufficient without such complications as were contributed by a Pennsylvania justice of the peace. A man wrote a will leaving all his possessions to his wife. He used an ordinary sheet of letter paper. His son took the will to the J. P. after the death of the testator who said it should be in legal form, wrote it out on a legal blank, clipped the signature from the original, and pasted it on the blank. Fortunately, the original had not been lost, and after examination of the two documents, the will was admitted to probate. The irony of fate, at least, in so far as the J. P. was concerned lies in the fact that the original will was drawn by a doctor.

* * *

One of Philadelphia's prominent colleges was founded from the bequests of a large fortune. The gift was made on the condition that, "No priest or minister of the Gospel should ever enter the grounds." Visitors for a time were usually asked if they came within this prohibited class so that it might appear that the college authorities were doing their best to observe this strange condition.

* * *

Obed Gardner's Will

Siasconset, May the 30th, 1841.

I, Obed Gardner, master mariner, now living at 'Sconset, write down this will.

Item.—I have cruised with my wife, Huldy Jane since 1811. We signed articles in town before the preacher on Independence Day. I want her and my oldest boy Jotham to be Captain and mate in bringin to port whatever I leave and to see that every one of the crew gets the lay as writ down on this paper. I put mother in command. I know shell be Captain any way, for six months after we started on our cruise I found out that I was mate and she was master. I dont mean that she ever mutinied, but I no that whenever we didnt agree she always manoovered to work to windward. May be it was all right for she could sail closer to wind than I could and could manage the crew of little ones that she had as much to do with shippin as I did. She always wanted me to do the swearin when there was any trubble. I no that when she and Jotham break bulk the cargo will be got out as well as I could do it myself.

Item.—In 1838 Captain Ichabod Worth got tired of the old Nancy Rotch and wanted to get rid of her so he got me to take a piece of her. When I saw her last she was lyin at the wharf in Valparaiso moren half full. I mean she was moren half full of oil. Mother never liked her. I want Jotham to have that piece as extra pay for what he does in settlin up my affairs for heel have to steer things while mother is takin observations, watchin the weather and lookin over things below decks.

Item.—I want mother to have the house on Union Street until she goes aloft. Then I want it to go to the children in equal lays and if any child dies I want the lay of the parent to go to the parents young ones. But I dont want my daughter Belindy to have anything as long as her husband is livin. He is a lubber, but she has been cruisin with him for years. I havent got anything agin him but he doesnt no how to navigate the sea of life. I do believe if he wanted to stop a leak board ship it would be just like him to go into the hold with an auger and bore a hole threw the plankin to let the bilge water out into the sea. But Belindy likes him. Thats just like a woman. If I should give the lay out and out to her, I am afraid her husband would manoover to get hold of it. So I want mother and Jotham to put it out at interest and give what comes out of it to her until her husband ships for a corpse below decks in the grave yard. Then she can take the lay and do what she wants to with it.

Item.—I dont want my son Ezry to have anything from what I leave. All the children except him was good ones. They looked out for mother and me. He didnt take after either of us except the time he took after me with a fid and hit me over the starboard eye. He new what was to come and was smart enough to jump into Johnny Gibbs catboat, haul in the sheet and steer for the continent. When he got to Bedford he shipped as boat steerer on the old Falcon. I was glad he did. I dont know where he is now but I herd he was master of a steamboat runnin between Canton and Whampoa. I havent got any use of him and I guess he hasnt got any for me. The black eye he gave me is outlawed and I dont now lay anything up agin him, for that.

Item.—I want mother and Jotham to settle up things as soon as they can, break bulk and make a fair divide between the children. But dont forget what I have writ down about mother and Belindy. I dont think Belindys husband will make any fuss about the way I have taken care of her unless she runs head on the shoals of a lawyers office. Then look out for squalls. I hope sheel stand off if she sees a lawyer comin thort her bows.

Item.—I want mother to have half of what comes from what is left of my property besides the house in Union Street. She deserves it. Every time I was around the Horn she did her duty to the young ones and I want her to have enough to live on until she goes aloft. Then I want her lay to go to the children in equal pieces except that Belindy shall only have what comes from it until her husband dies. If mother wants to marry again thats her business. I never did like to cruise without a mate, and I guess she wouldnt like to either.

OBED GARDNER
Master Mariner.

Captain Obed Gardner ast us into his porch and opened his locker. He then ast us to take a drink of rum that was fetched to him from Boston by Captain George Swain, in his schooner. We done so. It was masterly warmin to our insides. Then he pulled this paper out of his pea jacket and signed it and said it was his will and he ast us to sign it as witnesses. We done so, then he ast one of us to write down what took place and as they said I was more of a skoller than they, I did so.

JETHRO COFFIN 2nd.
ELEASUR PADDACK.
SHUBAEL STARBUCK.

FAMOUS WILLS

WASHINGTON'S WILL
Describing his attitude towards slavery is commented on in this chapter.

NAPOLEON'S WILL
In which he portrays his attitude towards the English nation.

SHAKESPEARE'S WILL
The quaint and curious style of his period.

Other wills of historic personages make this short chapter well worth your perusal.

CHAPTER SEVEN

Famous Wills

GEORGE WASHINGTON made elaborate provisions to liberate all his slaves on his wife's death. He explains that: "To emancipate them during her life would, though earnestly wished by me, be attended with such insuperable difficulties on account of their intermixture by marriage with the dower negroes, as to excite the most painful sensations, if not disagreeable consequences from the latter, while both descriptions are in occupancy of the same proprietor; it not being in my power, under the tenure by which the dower negroes are held, to manumit them."

* * *

Napoleon's will contains some striking passages:

> "I die prematurely, assassinated by the English oligarchy. The English nation will not be slow in avenging me.
>
> "The two unfortunate results of the invasions of France, when she still has so many resources are to be attributed to the treason of Marmont, Augerau, Talleyrand and La Fayette.
>
> "I forgive them,—may the posterity of France forgive them like me.
>
> "I disavow the 'Manuscript of Helena' and other works under the title of 'Maxims, Sayings, Etc.,' which persons have been pleased to publish for the last six years. These are not the rules which have guided my life. I caused the Duc d'Enghien to be arrested and tried because that step was essential to the safety, interest, and honor of the

French people, when the Count d'Artois was maintaining by his confession, sixty assassins at Paris. Under similar circumstances, I would act in the same way."

* * *

Shakespeare's Will

Shakespeare commences his will as follows:

"In the name of God, Amen. I, William Shakespeare, of Stratford-on-Avon, in the county of Warwick, gent., in perfect health and memory (God be praised!) do make and ordain this my last will and testament in manner and form following: that is to say: First, I commend my soul into the hands of God, my creator, hoping, and assuredly believing, through the only merits of Jesus Christ my Saviour, to be made partaker of life everlasting; and my body to the earth whereof it is made. Item, I give and bequeath unto my daughter Judith, £150, to be paid to her in manner following: £100 in discharge of her marriage portion, and £50 upon her surrendering all her right in one copyhold tenement in Stratford-on-Avon unto my daughter Susanna Hall and her heirs forever. Item, I give to my daughter Judith £150 more if she or any issue of her body be living at the end of three years next ensuing, the date of this my will. . . . Item, I given and bequeath to Hamlett Sadler 26s. 8d. to buy him a ring; to William Reynolds, gent., 26s. 8d. to buy him a ring; to my godson William Walker, 20s. in gold; to Anthony Nash, gent., 26s. 8d., and to Mr. John Nash 26s. 8d., and to my fellows John Hemynge, Richard Barbage, and Henry Candell, 26s. 8d. to buy them rings. . . . Item, I give unto my wife my second best bed with the furniture. . . . All the rest of my goods . . . I give to my son-in-law John Halls, gent. and my daughter Susanna his wife, whom I make executors, . . . and I do entreat and appoint Thomas Russell, Esq., and Francis Collins, gent., to be overseers hereof. . . ."

John Randolph, "Randolph of Roanoke," gave all his slaves their freedom, "heartily regretting that I have ever been the holder of one," and provided a sum not exceeding $8000 "to transport and settle said slaves to and in some other state or territory of the United States, giving to all above the age of forty not less than ten acres of land to each." In a codicil to Randolph's will, his classic statement is contained:

> "As lawyers and courts of law are extremely addicted to making wills for dead men, which they never made when living, it is my will and desire that no person who shall set aside, or attempt to set aside, the will above referred to, shall ever inherit, possess, or enjoy any part of my estate, real or personal."

* * *

Thomas Jefferson and Robert E. Lee also provided for the liberation of their slaves. Chief Justice Marshall, after directing the freeing of his body servant, provided that "If such emancipation should not be consistent with law, Robin might select his future owner from the testator's sons and daughters."

* * *

Benjamin Franklin begins his will with an elaborate introduction of himself as "printer, late Minister Plenipotentiary from the United States of America to the Court of France, now President of Pennsylvania," and bequeathed his "fine crab-tree walking stick, with gold head, curiously wrought, in the form of the cap of Liberty" to his friend and the friend of mankind, George Washington. He left 100 pounds to the free schools of Boston, from which fund the well-known Franklin medals are given to scholars of the high schools, and 1000 pounds each to Boston and Philadelphia to help young married artificers under the age of twenty-five. It was this latter fund which has figured in repeated litigation in the courts of Pennsylvania and Massachuetts.

* * *

Alexander Hamilton drew his will fearful that his estate would prove insufficient to discharge his debts, and entreated his children to make good any deficiency:

> "Though conscious that I have too far sacrificed the interests of my family to public avocations, and on this account have the less claim to burthen my children, yet I trust in their magnanimity to appreciate as they ought, this my request."

* * *

Paul Revere cut off his grandson Frank, "who now writes his name Francis" with one dollar.

* * *

Senator Sherman, the author of the anti-trust law, directed that within two years of his death, his books and papers were to be placed in the hands of some competent person who should "preface and publish an impartial biography of me with selections of my speeches and writings." Ten thousand dollars was set aside for that purpose and the testator explains that this is done "not to secure an eulogy, for I am conscious of many faults, but I claim that in my duty to the public, I have been honest, faithful and true."

* * *

Martin Van Buren begins a will full of domestic affairs, yet carefully conceived and well-drawn, by explaining that he has been "heretofore Governor of the

State, and more recently President of the United States, but for the last and happiest years of my life, a farmer in my native town."

* * *

Daniel Webster expressed:

> "My great and leading wish is to preserve Marshfield, if I can, in the blood and name of my own family. To this end, it must go in the first place to my son, Fletcher Webster, who is hereafter to be the immediate prop of my house, and the general representative of my name and character."

* * *

Lord Nelson dates his will "October 21, 1805, in full sight of the combined fleets of France and Spain, distance about two miles," and asks the royal favor for Emma, Lady Hamilton.

* * *

Dean Swift, in a long and elaborate will, among other legacies, left his third best beaver hat and his horses to his friend the Reverend John Jackson, Vicar of Santry, "lamenting that I had not credit enough with any Chief Governor (since the change of times) to get some additional Church Preferment for so virtuous and worthy a gentleman."

* * *

Voltaire left a note endorsed "Mon Testament," which on being opened, exhibited these lines in his own hand:

> "Je meurs en adorant Dieu,
> En aimant mes amis,
> En ne haissant point mes ennemis,
> En Detestant la superstition."

STRANGE PARCHMENTS

WITNESS *the will tattooed on the back of a beautiful young lady which is discussed in this chapter. A book has been written from the incidents that occurred at the execution of this instrument, and in accordance with the best theme of fiction, the young lady actually married the chief beneficiary of this strange will.*

Other strange places for the execution of wills are disclosed in this chapter.

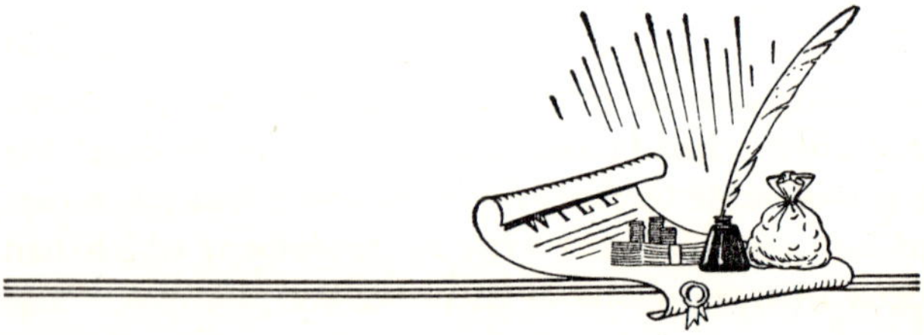

CHAPTER EIGHT

Strange Parchments

SOME persons choose singular objects on which to inscribe their last wills. Perhaps the choice place, at least in so far as law professors love to tell their students, is the back of a beautiful young lady. This was the case in the instance of the legend that a wealthy individual was ship-wrecked along with companions on an uninhabited island. With no writing materials available, a sailor volunteered to tattoo the will on the back of a young woman companion to which the testator made his mark.

* * *

In England a recluse wrote his will, while too weak to contact human aid, upon the corner of a bedpost.

* * *

A midwestern farmer laboriously traced his will in paint on the rough walls of a corn bin.

* * *

One of the most outstanding examples of strange parchments involves a California will, purporting to bequeath the estate of an eccentric who had amassed a considerable fortune. A few months after his death, and after it had become known that the deceased left a considerable fortune, two nurses who had taken care of him came forward with an instrument which had been written by one of them on her petticoat. The testimony established that the testator was too weak to write, and that he signed the will by making a cross, and the two beneficiaries signed as witnesses. The will left the bulk of the estate to a relative of the testator, but gave $10,000 each to the two nurses who had served him during his last illness. One singularity about this will was the fact that the petticoat bearing the will was hung in a closet unwashed or worn again and entirely forgotten about until one of the nurses remembered, after the death of the testator, the circumstances under which the will was written.

Strange as the circumstances surrounding this will were, a jury found that the will was genuine, supplanting an instrument in the custody of a reputable bank. As a matter of law, however, the nurses did not share in the estate, since they were witnesses to the will. The case was finally settled out of court and appeals were dismissed, but subsequently, the nurses started suit against the principal legatee on the grounds that they had received only $2,000 of the $10,000 promised them for their services as witnesses in the court should the will be held to be genuine.

* * *

The rung of a stepladder was the object used in one case in which a probate was denied on the grounds that it was a forgery. Here again, a deathbed friend and companion—this time also a nurse, was the chief beneficiary. The sob story that she told in trying to establish this will runs along the usual lines. The testator loved her greatly and the will, drawn according to the usual methods, was not good enough for her, according to the enraptured feelings of the testator. He looked around for peculiar places in which to write the will and finally hit upon the stepladder, signifying a rise to higher things as the proper place for this important instrument.

It was established, however, by competent expert testimony that the handwriting was not that of the testator. As in the celebrated Hauptmann case, the testator was a German, and German characteristics are usually carried into the writing of other languages so as to make identification by an expert positive.

* * *

In practically all circumstances similar to the stepladder will, a California will was offered for probate, written upon a match box. The chief beneficiary was a neighbor woman who had taken care of the deceased and for whom, according to her testimony, the testator had the highest regard.

Here again the expert testimony wrecked the scheme. The alleged testator was of Spanish descent and the tell-tale foreign characteristics were absent from the purported will. In fact, it was written far better than the testator, a man of little education, had ever written in his life.

Here is a field of crime in which women excel, paricularly those who have made it a point to please men of property, whose expectations of life seem short.

* * *

A court was once called upon to decide whether a will left on a graphophone cylinder was valid, or whether the strange "last will and testament" should be disregarded in the settlement of the estate. A wealthy landowner died and after the funeral his heirs began to look for the will. Much to their surprise, they were unable to find the slightest trace of it. The missing document, however, was found in a few days in the strangest place imaginable. A young man happening to see a graphophone on a table in the library, put a record on it, which he supposed was that of some popular Russian song. To his amazement, however, instead of a song, he heard the dead man's voice recite the words of the missing will.

The heirs were notified of this discovery and they lost no time in examining the record containing the will. It was found to be flawless.

* * *

In Buffalo several months ago a will was probated on the back of a prescription blank.

* * *

Tragic the setting of the will of the dying brakeman, victim of a train wreck who scribbled the words "my wife to have all" on the back of a route card torn from an overturned box car. Great the spiritual value of his offering however small his estate when we consider that the wife he left behind was consoled with the knowledge that even as death was rushing forward with out-stretched arms, her welfare was the thought that flashed through his mind.

* * *

The fly leaves of many a family bible have contained the wills of many of our ancestors. In a modern world this would seem a strange place. It is to be remembered however, that paper was scarce in our early history and not available in every household.

An examination of these wills written on "The Book of Books" discloses that in almost every instance these wills begin with an expression of the abiding faith of the testator in his or her creator. This can be explained in part by the fact that in those solid times religion was a major moving force in all activity. But be that as it may, the parchment on which these last wills were written must have had a steadying influence on the disposition of the worldly goods in accordance with the mandates of religious ardor.

Indeed within the memory of living men the practice of commencing the will with an expression of religious sentiment has been common and in the so-called "Bible Belts" wills written in the family Bibles have quite recently been admitted to probate.

* * *

An interesting bit of Americana is reflected in some wills of about fifty years ago which were written on pages torn from almanacks, recalling the period when the almanack served as guide to man and beast and also constituted about the only current publication with a country wide distribution.

* * *

True to their tradition to offer the customer everything obtainable from pins to steam engines, it has been reported that mail order catalogues have been used as the parchment for several wills.

ESTATE PLANNING

THE *rise of a new profession is heralded in this chapter on estate planning —a profession charged with a definite responsibility. How well the profession is meeting this responsibility may be gathered from the illuminating illustrations given from actual experiences of the author. Some of the perplexing problems of estate planning are frankly discussed.*

CHAPTER NINE

Estate Planning

As shown in the chapter on the history of wills, the age old cry of the testator since the first will was written on tablets of stone has been, "How can I leave to those near and dear to me the worldly goods with which I am endowed, secure in the knowledge that they will always have the benefit and use thereof." It is to be noted that the cry is for others. We came into this world without property; we leave this world without property. The years in the interim have brought property which we hold in trust for those we leave behind. Their welfare is the prime consideration when our will is drawn.

Every human need finally brings into existence a profession whose ethics are devoted to filling that need. And so it is with estate planning.

Estate planning, as we now know it, is of comparatively recent origin. It is the result of ever-growing complications and diversified corporate interests oft times located in various states, varying laws of descent and distribution, and probably the greatest of all—Federal and State tax burdens. Estate planning should be designed to the end that beneficiaries will receive their heritage in a manner by which they are best served, and with the least possible losses from dissipation of principal and shrinkage, due to fluctuating business conditions and to the ever-growing appetite of the tax collector. Anomalous as the statement may seem, estate planning is not and cannot be the sole accomplishment of any individual. Modern complexity of society has seen to that.

An efficiently planned estate requires the services of a lawyer, tax consultant, accountant, trust officer, and life insurance underwriter. Each profession in itself is a full-time occupation. The function of an estate planner is to correlate these various services. Obviously, a proficient estate planner must have a thorough working knowledge of the functions of these various professions.

The advice of anyone of these, while valuable when considered in relation to its bearing on the problem of the particular field, must be discounted as to problems which occur in other fields. Naturally, certain problems cut across other fields and some general knowledge of other fields is necessary to properly advise as to problems in individual fields. It is an entirely different matter, however, to correlate the advice of experts in all fields, and to tie together, so to speak, the ends so that there will have merged from the numerous threads a complete pattern woven into an harmonious design which must take place before the well-planned estate can take its final form. This tying together and weaving of a final pattern is the function of an estate planner.

Estate planning as far as this author is concerned was born some seventeen years ago. This birth was not without extreme mental anguish. As an officer of a local trust company, it was his sole duty to persuade the clients of the company to appoint a bank as their executor and trustee. "A trust company is better qualified," was about all we had to offer.

One day, one of our leading Directors complained

bitterly, stating that eighty per cent of all will appointments secured for the bank would be changed within two years. The obvious conclusion was, unless the appointee died within a few months, these appointments would either be lost to the Bank or would have to be secured over and over again. The author blithely suggested, which suggestions almost cost him his job, that he believed that men seldom changed anything that satisfied them; while, on the one hand, men were always ready and seeking to change anything that dissatisfied them. Therefore, if these men's wills were properly worked out, to the extent of complete satisfaction, the mortality of these appointments would be reduced from eighty per cent to a nominal per cent. This statement so enraged this director that for a few moments—which few moments seemed almost an eternity—the author was sure of being fired immediately. But after due deliberation, he was directed to solve the problem—"or else"—

The solution is too long a story to be an interesting one. In brief, the author discovered a "fundamental key," which always provides the basis for the solution of the planning of any estate, notwithstanding the fact that no two estates are ever the same.

Countless numbers of his clients, attorneys, tax consultants, trust officers, and others with whom he has worked, have told him that this "key" readily solves the problem.

The use of this "key" is empirical. It requires judgment, and judgment is always born of experience. Seventeen years of experience, during which time the author has planned estates totaling several hundred millions of dollars, is a step in that direction.

In the planning of one's estate, *changes* must be anticipated.

I. Beneficiaries may change due to birth or death.

II. Men's fortunes invariably increase or decrease, requiring change of distributions, based on these increases or decreases.

III. It is also highly desirable that one's executors and trustees be vested with full powers, powers which will enable them to act for the best interest of the estate and at the same time, reasonably hold the executors and trustees accountable for their errors. A properly planned estate must provide for these changes, as and when they may occur.

Also tax avoidance—not tax evasion—should be practiced. The judiciary is the authority for this statement.

Justice Learned Hand of the Circuit Court of Appeals said:

> "Anyone may so arrange his affairs that taxes shall be as low as possible; he is not bound to choose that pattern which will best pay the treasury; it is not even a patriotic duty to increase one's taxes." (Helvering v. Gregory, 69 Fed. (2d) 809.)

In affirming the above case, the Supreme Court held:

> "The legal right of a taxpayer to decrease the amount of what otherwise would be his taxes, or to altogether avoid them by means which the law permits, cannot be doubted." (Gregory v. Helvering, 293 U. S. 465.)

To the uninitiated, all of this may seem a very complicated matter. In reality, a properly planned estate greatly simplifies matters, and a planned estate is always "in gear" with changing conditions.

One of the most interesting and comprehensive pictures of the value of planned estates was given the author by a friend in Boston, Mass., some years ago.

Knowing the author's interest in these matters, he told of his collection of newspaper accounts of many thousands of persons, many of them wives and daughters, who had been left financially comfortable and in numerous instances had received large fortunes, yet these same persons, in a few years, were destitute.

"Doubtless, you too, from time to time, have seen similar accounts in the news items," he querried.

He continued, "The shame of this frightful picture is simply this. These situations were, in almost every instance, entirely avoidable. With us New Englanders—it is the rule, rather than the exception, that estates in this section are passed to wives, sons and daughters, and other beneficiaries, in such a manner that the beneficiaries live to enjoy their heritages, not to regret them."

"I believe it is the duty and obligation of every husband and every father to give enough time and thought to the planning of his affairs, to provide that when his estate is passed to his loved ones, it is passed in such a manner, that they will be helped, and not harmed. I further believe," he continued, "that each and every man should plan for reasonable comfort for himself and his wife in what should be his most comfortable years, the twilight of life."

He remarked, "I believe that we can all agree that a person born blind does not realize the loss of his sight, nearly as much as a person who loses his sight after reaching manhood."

"And by the same token, does not a person accustomed to reasonable comforts suffer more, upon the loss of these comforts, than one who has never been so fortunate?"

Judged by estate planning standards, people fall into one of three general classes:

1. Those who have no interest in planning their affairs.
2. Those who defer planning until they believe they have reached their goal and accumulated a substantial fortune.
3. Those who "plan" what they now have, and in addition, "plan" what they may later acquire.

As to the first two classes, they are respectfully referred to the advice of the author's friend from Boston.

In many instances, Life Insurance forms a considerable portion of many estates. Yet, it is generally true that few have taken full advantage of all the benefits their insurance can guarantee, either to the insured or to the beneficiaries.

Seventeen years of planning estates has not been without its interesting experiences. A few of these experiences are briefly given and for obvious reasons, the identity of these parties is not revealed.

When Foresight Paid

Some years ago, some young people inherited outright from a relative about $2,000,000. After a considerable amount of persuasion, these parties accepted the suggestion that the boys create an irrevocable trust with a trust company for themselves for a ten-year period; the girls create an irrevocable trust for half of their inheritance for their entire lives.

A few years ago one of these parties said that the only money he had left in the world—although he was previously wealthy—was the trust which he had set apart for himself, and which funds he would shortly receive.

Finding a Way

Sometime ago, when planning the estate of a party who was operating what might be well termed "a one-man business," the author learned that this client was directed by his father's will to pay his mother $1,000 a month. This obligation was a source of considerable worry, especially should he predecease his mother. He stated that he had considered life insurance, but he could not afford to carry between $300,000 and $400,000 of insurance to guarantee this protection to his mother. The author recommended a seldom-used insurance contract, which provided upon his death for the payment of $1,000 to his mother as long as she lived, and the premium rate for this contract was less than one-third of what he had expected to pay. As this contract seemed altogether too true to him, he submitted it to his attorney who in turn submitted it to the firm's New York City bankers, and this contract was finally accepted. The New York City banker's comment was, "If we didn't know the reliability of the Company behind this insurance, we wouldn't believe it."

A Living Trust

Another client, "in the good old days," sold a portion of his holdings to the public. He was advised to create two living Trusts with his Trust Company, one for himself and another for his family and in addition, to purchase a Single Premium Life policy, without "Incidents of Ownership," for his family.

Notwithstanding the reverses which this Corporation has suffered, in common with many other Corporations, this party and his family have no financial worries.

Solving the Estate Tax Problem

Another client, being faced with a large Inheritance Tax, created irrevocable Trusts for his dependents with his Trust Companies, and in addition divested himself of "Incidents of Ownership" of a goodly portion of his Life Insurance, with the net result that his Inheritance Taxes have been reduced by many thousands of dollars.

Reducing Insurance

Another client was carrying considerable insurance—a line of some $350,000. Realizing this client's business was facing fundamental changes and further realizing that he was borrowing on this insurance to pay for it, together with the fact that he had only one beneficiary, he was advised to reduce his insurance from $350,000 to $100,000 or $150,000, and to use the cash value of the cancelled insurance to prepay his remaining insurance for at least fifteen years. Unfortunately, this advice was not followed. Today, this party is struggling to keep $35,000 of insurance in force.

Paying Its Way

A manufacturer, involved together with his family in many different industries, was carrying all of the insurance payable to his estate. He was advised to create an insurance trust for his family with a part of this insurance and the balance of his insurance he assigned to the bank, his largest creditor. As the bank was better protected by this plan, they reduced his interest rate by one per cent, which reduction was about enough to pay for the premiums on his family's insurance. Thus, he definitely protected his family and his principal creditor.

A Problem of Distribution

Sometime ago, a woman who was over sixty, inherited a substantial sum from a relative. She was faced with two problems, the safe investment of these funds, and the realization that her sisters and brothers were less well off than she was. With approximately one-third of her inheritance, she purchased Annuities for herself which yield her an income equal to the income on her entire inheritance and with the remaining two-thirds of her inheritance, she created a living Trust with her Trust Company for her sisters and brothers.

Where Other Methods Fail

An outright sale of a very large industry brought considerable wealth to several men. One of these parties who received over two million dollars refused to plan his estate. With the greatest of reluctance, he consented to purchase $100,000 of life insurance. This client then ventured into new businesses, unknown to him. Although his death occurred only a few years after the sale, the $100,000 of life insurance was all the estate his widow received. Everything else, including his home, was lost.

Amortization

Upon arranging a loan at the bank for a client to buy some new equipment on which he could earn twenty per cent net, it seems wise to arrange with the banker to carry insurance against this loan. If he was making twenty per cent, he could better afford to pay eight per cent interest—the extra two per cent being the premium cost—so that if he died, the loan would be paid, than to pay six per cent without this protection. Reluctantly, he consented to this arrangement and within a year, this loan was paid at this party's death.

Providing for a Beloved Wife

Another client asked for some suggestions for the planning of his estate. He wanted to leave that portion which his wife would receive, outright to her. The author suggested that he trustee with his Trust Company as much of his estate as would reasonably guarantee to his wife the minimum income he wished her to have. At first, the author was curtly told that his wife was over fifty years of age, and that the idea was preposterous. After discussion, this party consented to this arrangement. Several years after this party's death, the widow said that the investments which she had made had depreciated about ninety per cent, but that her husband's trust still pays her $25,000 a year.

"If I Only Had—"

Recently the author met a former client, once a prosperous manufacturer—now reduced to a white collar job on one of the government projects. Although ten years had elapsed since our last business interview, the recommendations made at that time still stood out in that man's mind even though they were forgotten by the author. He recalled that he had turned down recommendations that he create a living trust for himself and his wife. Tragic was his closing statement, "If I only had," after he had informed the author that he had lost every cent and that his present indebtedness was in excess of $200,000.

These illustrations, a few of the actual experiences, of the author have been gathered from the busy stream of life. They illustrate the uncertainties of the future. Should they teach the lesson that only a scientifically planned estate can escape the devastating effects of unforeseen happenings, with attending unhappiness, the author will be satisfied. In this regard it must be ever remembered that each estate has its own peculiar problems which only the expert in these matters can successfully solve.

The title of this book, "To Will Or Not to Will," is not intended to convey the idea that estate planning is designed solely for the conservation of property after death. Proper estate planning, in addition to providing for the conservation of property after death, should also provide for one's advancing years, when the fireside, the pipe, and comforts become more alluring than the hurry and bustle of modern business demands.

In this equally important field, the estate planner contributes advice and counsel to those who desire these comforts for their later years in life.

* * *

In Recognition

No record of estate planning, however meager, could be complete without a tribute to the solid institutions whose services are freely utilized by the estate planner. Possibly, some day some one will record the Stewardship of the Trust Companies and the Life Insurance Companies. That they have been intrusted with many billions of dollars of property, is in itself, an eloquent tribute to their stewardship. This record is not equaled anywhere in the world.

* * *

> *"It marks a big step in a man's development when he comes to realize that other men can be called in to help him do a better job than he can do alone."*
>
> —ANDREW CARNEGIE.